OPEN STUDIO

OPEN STUDIO

THE WORK OF
ROBERT A.M. STERN ARCHITECTS

Robert A.M. Stern

Edited by Shannon Hohlbein
and Peter Morris Dixon

The Monacelli Press

Library of Congress Control Number 2018951376
ISBN 978150935180

Front Cover:
RAMSA Office
New York, New York

Back Cover:
RAMSA Office
New York, New York

Endpapers:
City Grid
The Metropolitan Collection for Atlas Carpet Mills

Design by Pentagram

Printed in Singapore

The Monacelli Press
6 West 18th Street
New York, New York 10011

www.monacellipress.com

ROBERT A.M. STERN ARCHITECTS

FOUNDER AND SENIOR PARTNER
Robert A.M. Stern

PARTNERS
Gary L. Brewer
Randy M. Correll
Melissa DelVecchio
Sargent C. Gardiner
Preston J. Gumberich
Michael D. Jones
Alexander P. Lamis
Daniel Lobitz
Grant F. Marani
Meghan L. McDermott
Roger H. Seifter
Kevin M. Smith
Jennifer L. Stone
Paul L. Whalen
Graham S. Wyatt

15//7

Y PARTNERS AND THOSE WHO
work with us constitute a community built around a shared
passion for architecture as an art and a profession. I hope that
those who leaf through these pages will come away with an
appreciation of the diversity of our practice, the camaraderie of
our office culture, and the principles that underlie our commitment. I hope you will enjoy this book, which has no agenda except
to offer a glimpse into the methods of our studio—our design
process from drawings and models through to buildings and the
various details that give them character.

We take pleasure in architecture's capacity to provide settings
for the drama of daily life. We believe that every circumstance
has within it a magic for each of us to discover and realize:
a sunlit corner in a courtyard, a glimpse of nature in a dense
urban setting, whatever. These, not theories of literature or
fabrication or electronic communication, are the elements that

transform mere buildings into compelling architecture—that help lift lives to higher levels of awareness, that give the public the environmental pleasure it craves and deserves. Architecture is a technical discipline, but it is first and foremost an art. Buildings have to be useful, but they need to be much more—they need to be bearers of meaning, and they need to speak to the public. Our job is to create the settings for ritual, reflection, and revelation, to make magic out of the mundane.

Architecture has its own language to be sure, but that language cannot be private, cannot be exclusive to architects. While the relationship between those who design buildings and those who commission them is crucial, equally important to the conversation is the public, the too-often-neglected group who, though they may only experience buildings as tenants or from the outside, frequently surprise us with their responses and their preferences.

Ours is an international practice with strong roots in the United States and, especially, in our home city, New York. But wherever we work, context is paramount. It is our intention to modify, but not to disrupt, the physical or cultural conditions of the places in which we are asked to build. We prefer buildings that fit in even as they stand out—we reject bravura for its own sake. Every place has its own character, which we see as a stimulus to creative invention. To set a new building in a demanding context can push architects to a further place than they've ever imagined.

We stick to principles to stay free of faddishness, to be grounded in the present but committed to the future—to the design of buildings that will stand the test of time, that can be adapted to new uses. We cannot return to a lost past, but we can and should look at what went before. Ours is a struggle to recapture the values of the past in our architecture: can we match up today to what was built before mass production and digital fabrication? The past is not to be played with; it is all we have to believe in. Modernism was a self-referential stylistic movement based on rebellion against the past. It is now part of the past, a phase in history. Today, to be modern we must liberate ourselves from modernism's blinders—today architects must replace narrow narcissism with a respect for place and tradition. Nonetheless, history is too important to simply be repeated without evolving.

Speed is the price of our modern condition. But the more we rush around, the more we need places that anchor us, that help make it possible to catch our breath in order to survive. Architecture is not a trivial pursuit. It is a commitment, a lifelong path to the discovery of new things and the recovery of valuable things once known and now forgotten. Architecture constantly makes and remakes the world. It is a vital natural force, a compelling human activity, a constellation of possibilities, the best way humankind has yet devised to shape the world. We must invent and reaffirm, search and research, and above all take risks. To thrive as an architect, risks must be taken; but risks need not get in the way of time-honored principles. To ignore the basics is to condemn architecture to infantilism. The human capacity for imagination and invention is limitless—but at the core there are certain standards that always define quality.

The work on the following pages is the result of collaborative efforts of very many, led by the partners of our firm and colleagues at all levels of our practice, who have brought their experience, their values, and their creative imaginations to the table. Together, working from the shared principles that underpin all of our designs, we have been privileged to undertake a broad range of commissions, always with an understanding of architecture as a fine art, an art with a narrative purpose, an art that embraces human values. And with that, I will let our work, presented through the lens of the camera, speak for itself.

Robert A.M. Stern

From dashed-off, gestural sketches—often intended as quick communication tools among teammates and for clients—to fully realized compositions, we are committed to the art of drawing as an essential component of architectural creation. As we move forward step by step, we begin to work with digital representations in combination with hand drawing. The computer is a wonderful tool, but absent hand drawing, software tends to alienate designers from the specificity and intimacy that is fundamental to the relationship between hand, eye, and brain. The hand-to-eye connection internalizes an impression of the built environment in a way that can never be replicated. We celebrate hand drawing in a gallery in our office commons and in our day-to-day work.

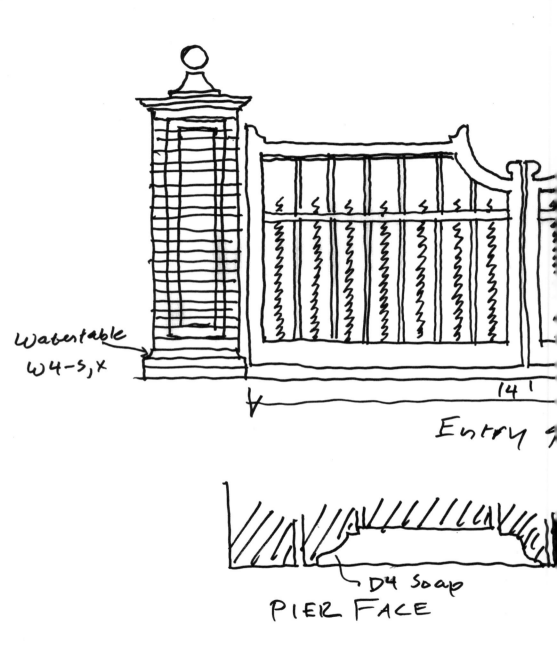

Watertable
W4-5,x

14'

Entry 9

D4 Soap

PIER FACE

PIER SIDE

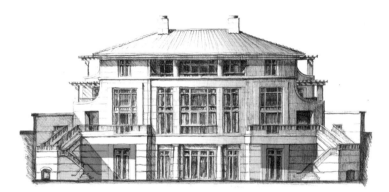

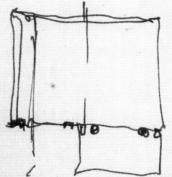

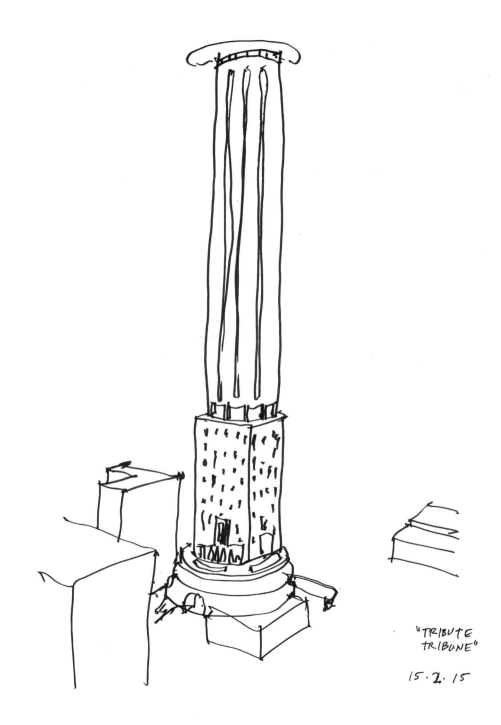

"TRIBUTE
TRIBUNE"

15.2.15

ROBERT A.M.
STERN
ARCHITECTS

A12 032.01
BARKLI MANSION
EXT. ELEV SKETCH
N.T.S.
9.25.2012
KEVIN SMITH

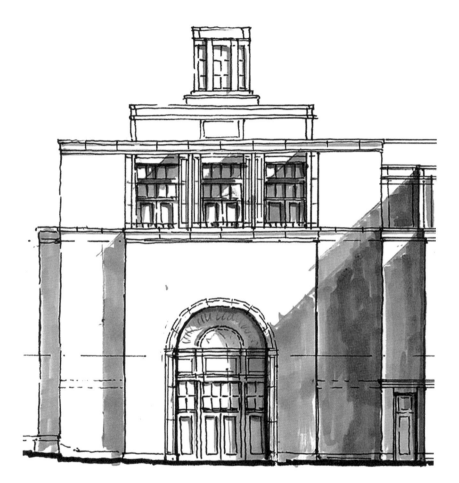

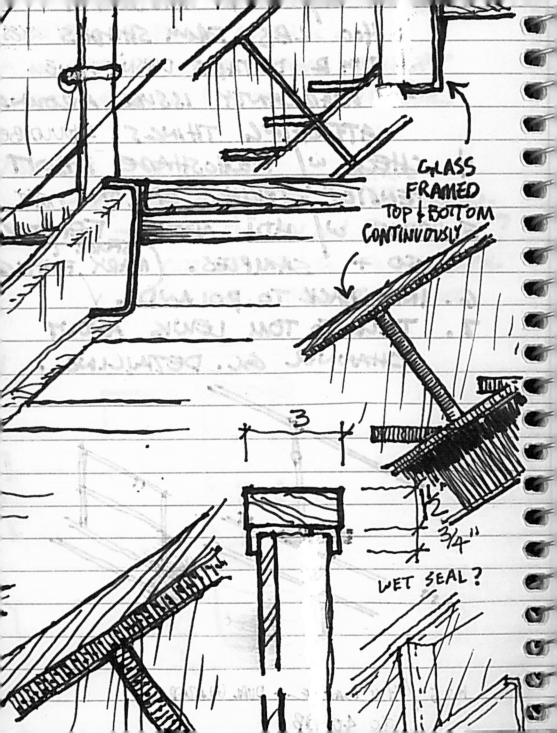

GLASS
FRAMED
TOP & BOTTOM
CONTINUOUSLY

3

1 1/2

3/4"

WET SEAL?

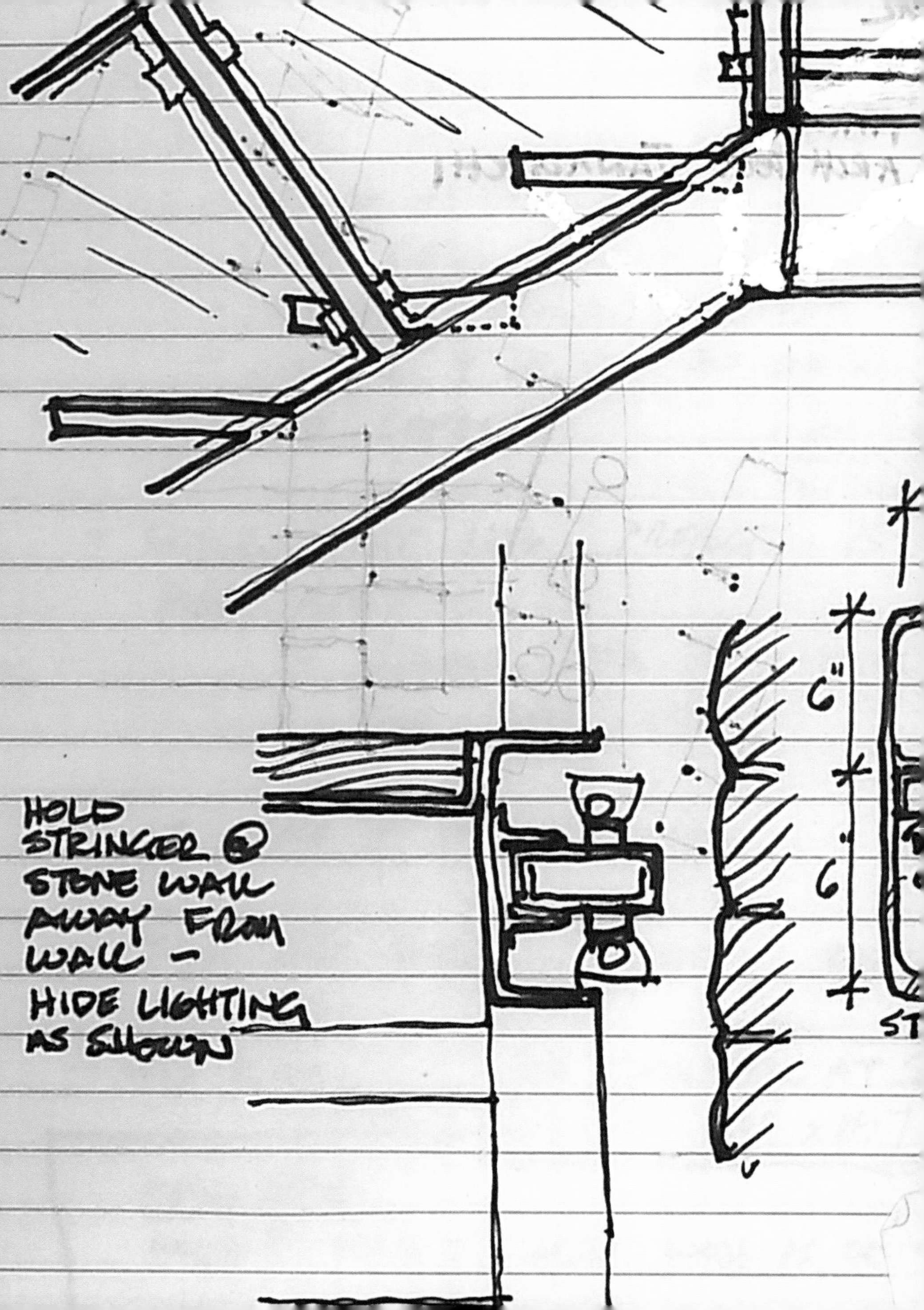

HOLD
STRINGER @
STONE WALL
AWAY FROM
WALL —
HIDE LIGHTING
AS SHOWN

6"

6"

ST

With the

arcades.

more charm!

"plain

softness"

panel

panel.

modified dome.

T 10 4
2 T 0 ?

1/3
straight

2013 / 3 /8.

RETAIL +336.

97 Church Street

Hotel Entr.

99 Church Hotel Entrance South Elev

4/11" = 1'-0

...lé Facade South Ele...

...l Facade- ...
West

4/16

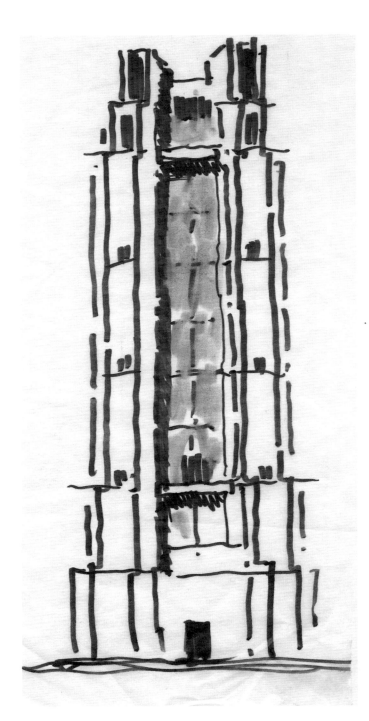

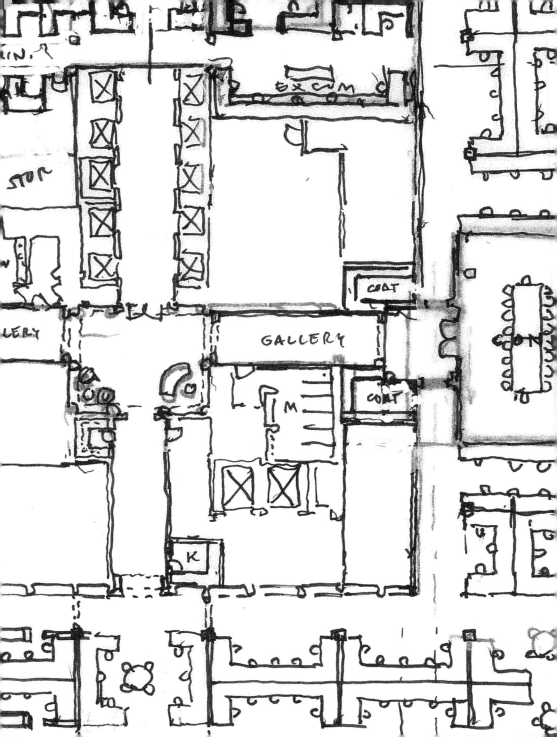

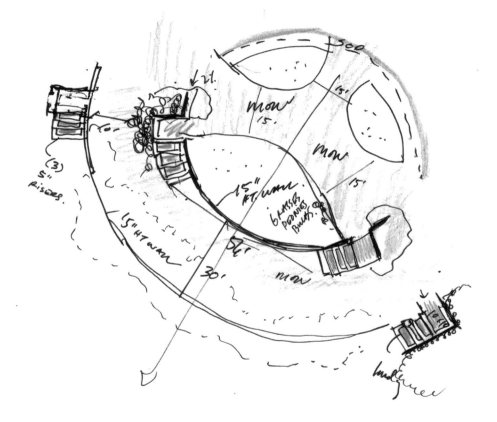

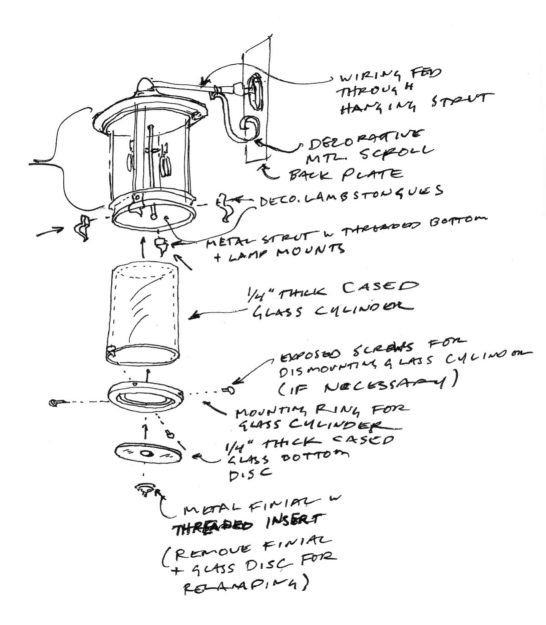

WIRING FED THROUGH HANGING STRUT

DECORATIVE MTL. SCROLL

BACK PLATE

DECO. LAMBSTONGUES

METAL STRUT w THREADED BOTTOM + LAMP MOUNTS

1/4" THICK CASED GLASS CYLINDER

EXPOSED SCREWS FOR DISMOUNTING GLASS CYLINDER (IF NECESSARY)

MOUNTING RING FOR GLASS CYLINDER

1/4" THICK CASED GLASS BOTTOM DISC

METAL FINIAL w THREADED INSERT

(REMOVE FINIAL + GLASS DISC FOR RELAMPING)

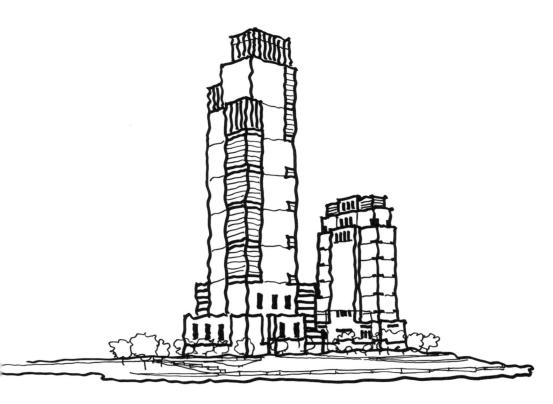

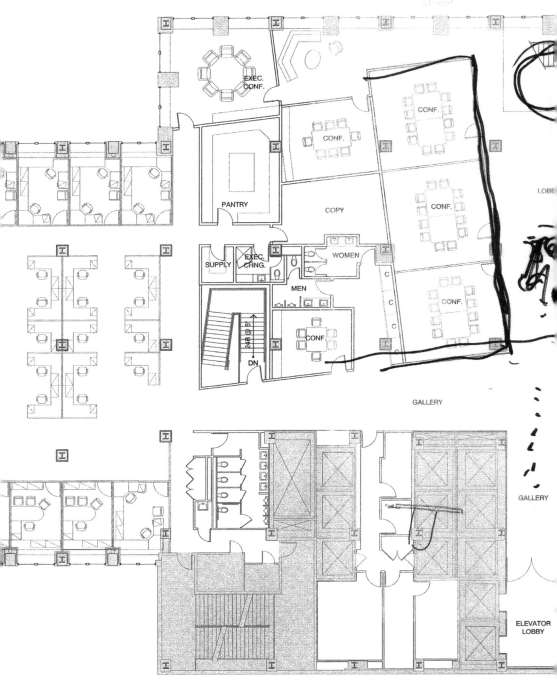

E. 47th
Street

EXEC. CONF.

CONF.

CONF.

CONF.

CONF.

LOBE

PANTRY

COPY

CONF.

SUPPLY

EXEC. CHNG.

WOMEN

MEN

C

C

C

24R @ 5"

DN

CONF.

CONF.

GALLERY

GALLERY

ELEVATOR LOBBY

E. 46th

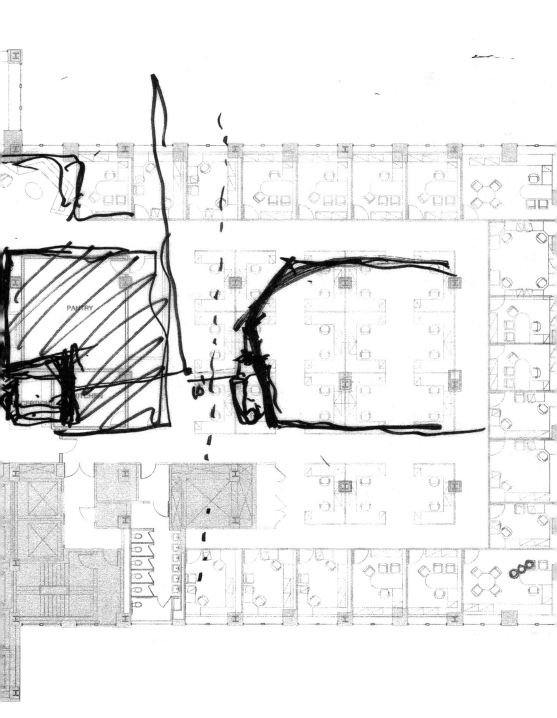

SOUTH ACADEMY ENTRY   2.5.15

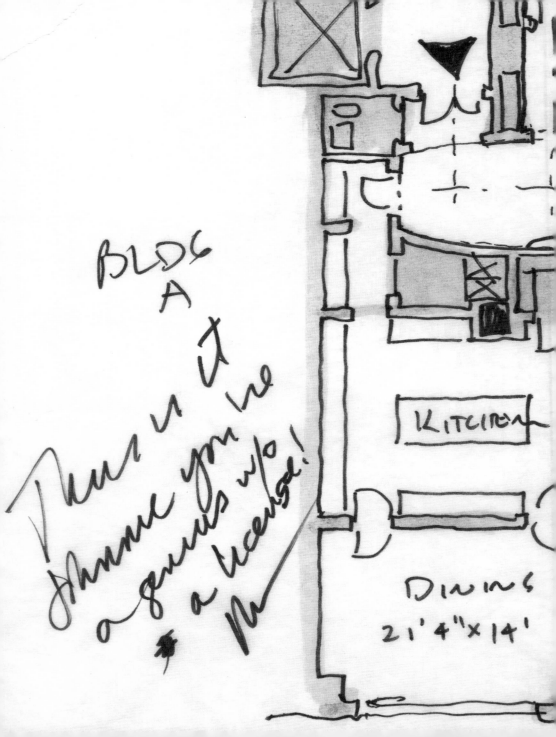

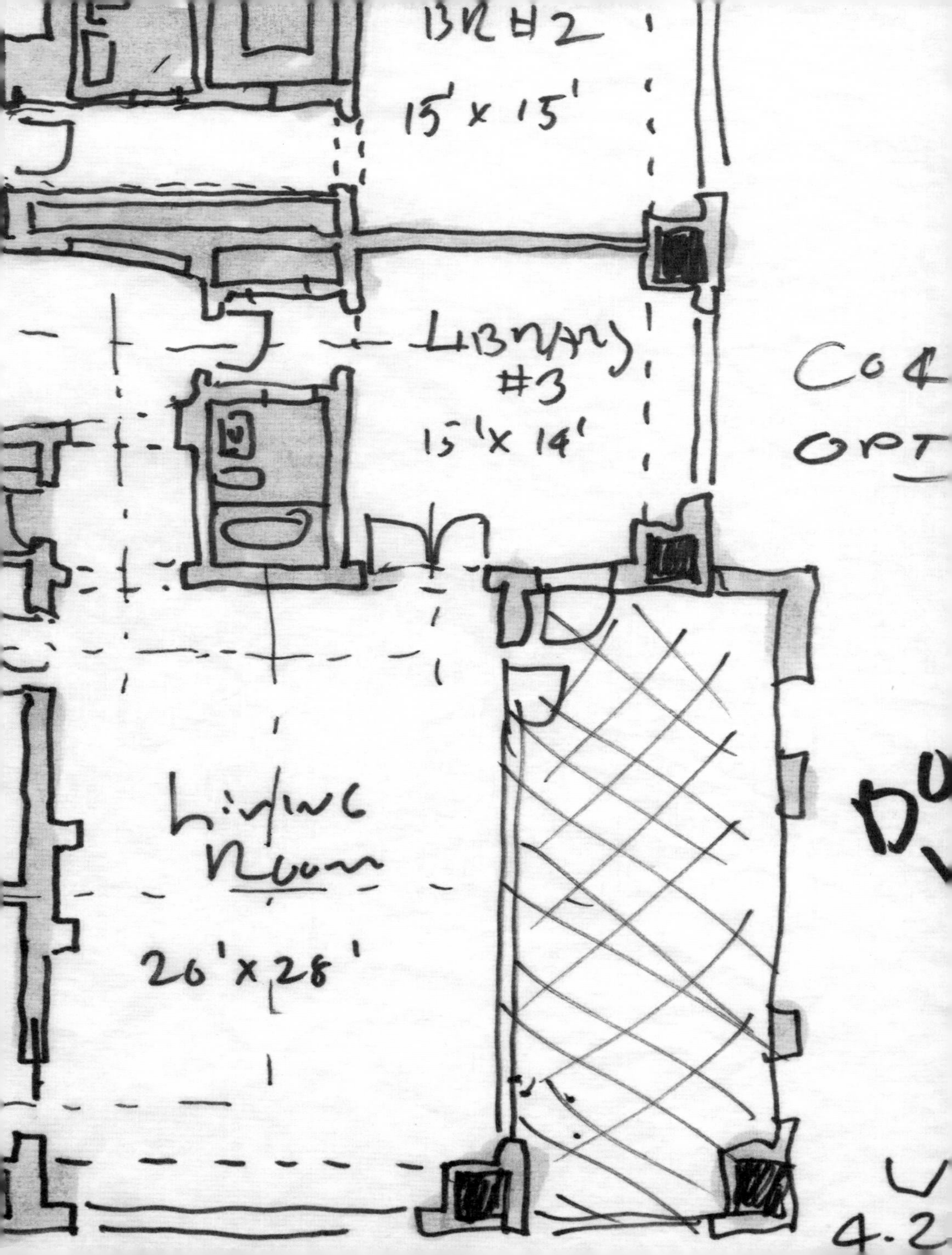

BR #2

15' x 15'

CO4

OPT

LIBRARY
#3
15' x 14'

LIVING
ROOM

26' x 28'

D

4.2

We remain committed to the art of model making, representing in three dimensions our design ideas as they evolve. Modeling clay enables us to think quickly—to sketch in three dimensions, as it were. Physical models using paper allow us to study our work at increasing scales and to consider critical details. And though we avail ourselves of the advantages of building information modeling, digital technology has not replaced the hands-on exploration that comes with physical modeling—leading in many instances to the resolution of geometries that exceed the capabilities of today's most sophisticated visualization software.

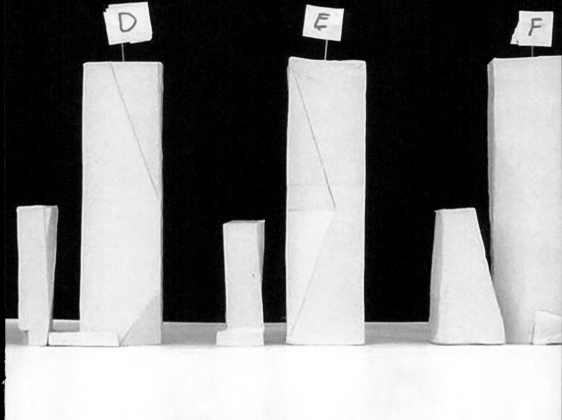

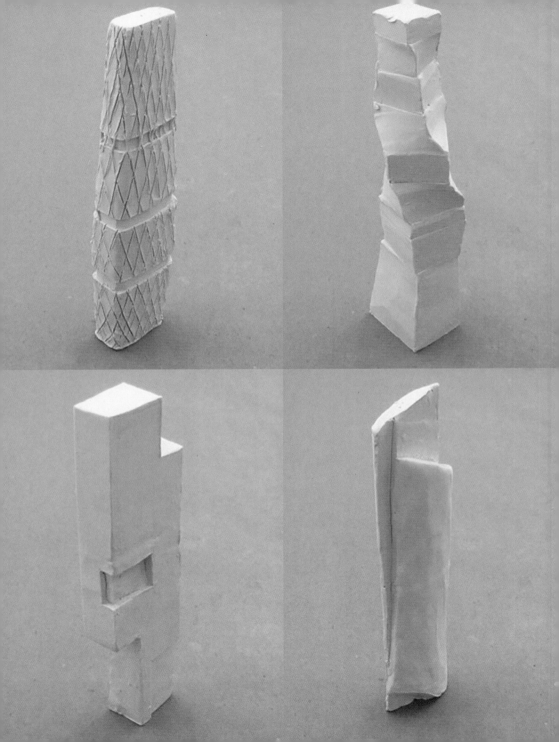

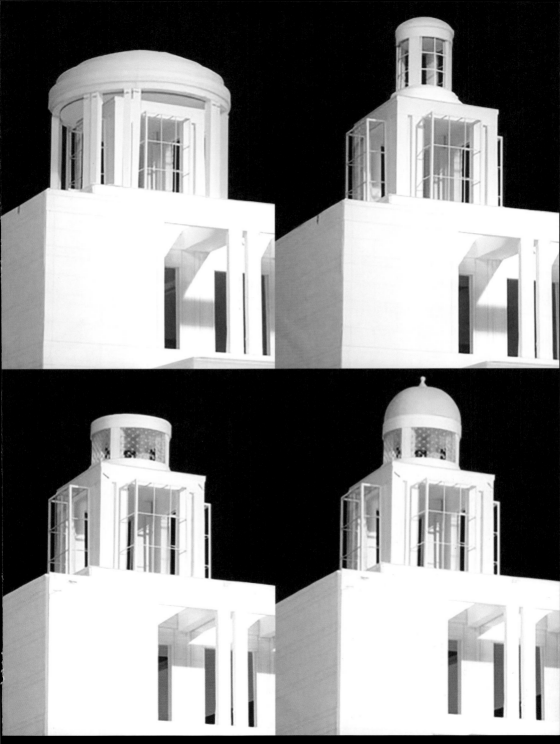

GHWA BASE OPTION
Scale: 1/32" = 1'-0"
2015-04-27

MAX BUILD OUT
Scale 1/32" = 1'-0"

RENDERING
AUGUST 05, 2014

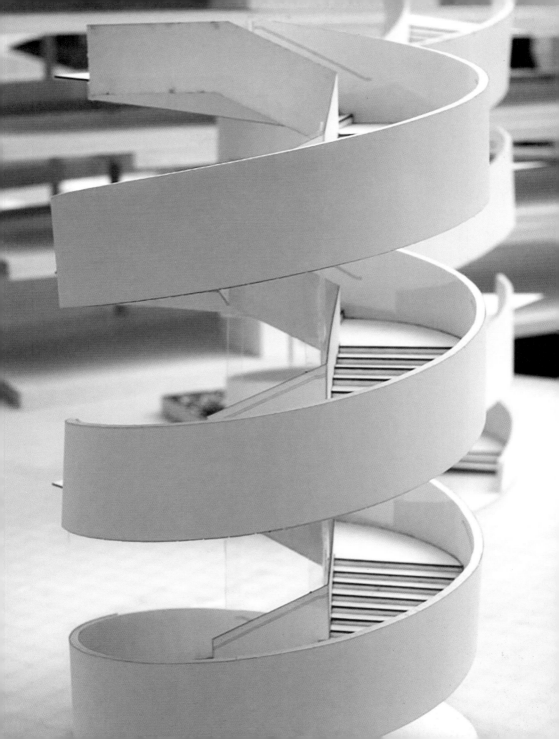

TOWER HEIGHT COMPARISON
YALE UNIVERSITY

SHEFFIELD STERLING
STRATHCONA HALL
186 FT

HALL OF GRADUATE STUDIES
189 FT

NORTH COLLEGE TOWER
195 FT

Architecture is not a solitary pursuit; our work is the result of collaborative creativity. The scale of our enterprise has grown. We are now sixteen partners—some of whom have been part of our leadership for a very long time—supported by a cadre of intelligent, energetic, and inquiring young minds attracted by our approach. This combination of experienced hands and new talents—whom we encourage to listen to everything that's going on, to wiggle their way into every meeting, and make themselves as useful as possible—bode well for the future. We are also indebted to innumerable professionals from related fields who enrich our work with their expertise, and we are grateful for the sympathetic collaboration and support of our many challenging clients from whom we always learn so much about the art of architecture and its possibilities.

14. Site Perspectives

...LITATION

10. Site Option 1 - Site Plan & Aerial Perspectives

REHABILITATION

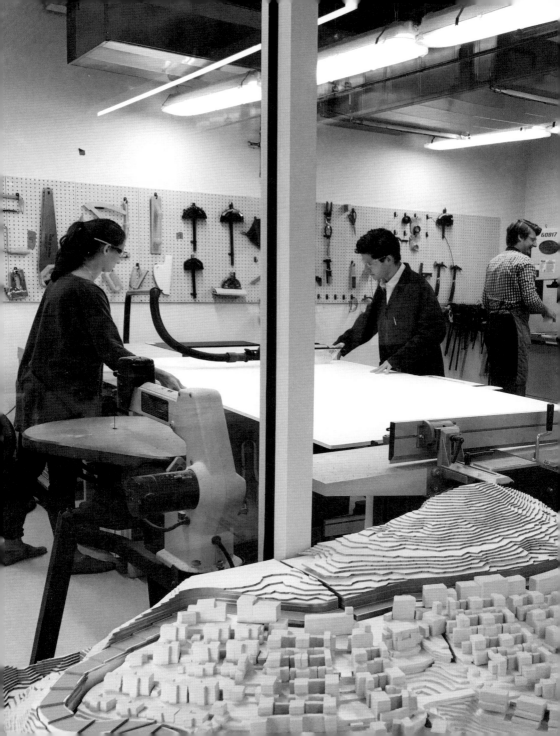

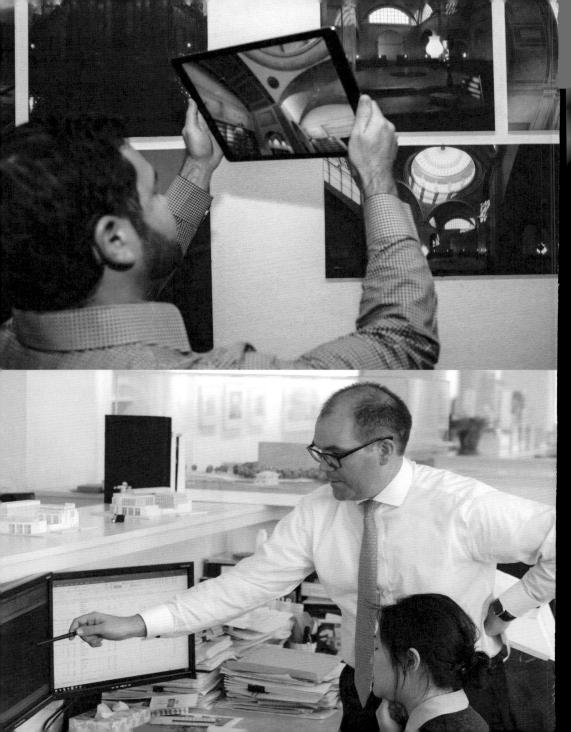

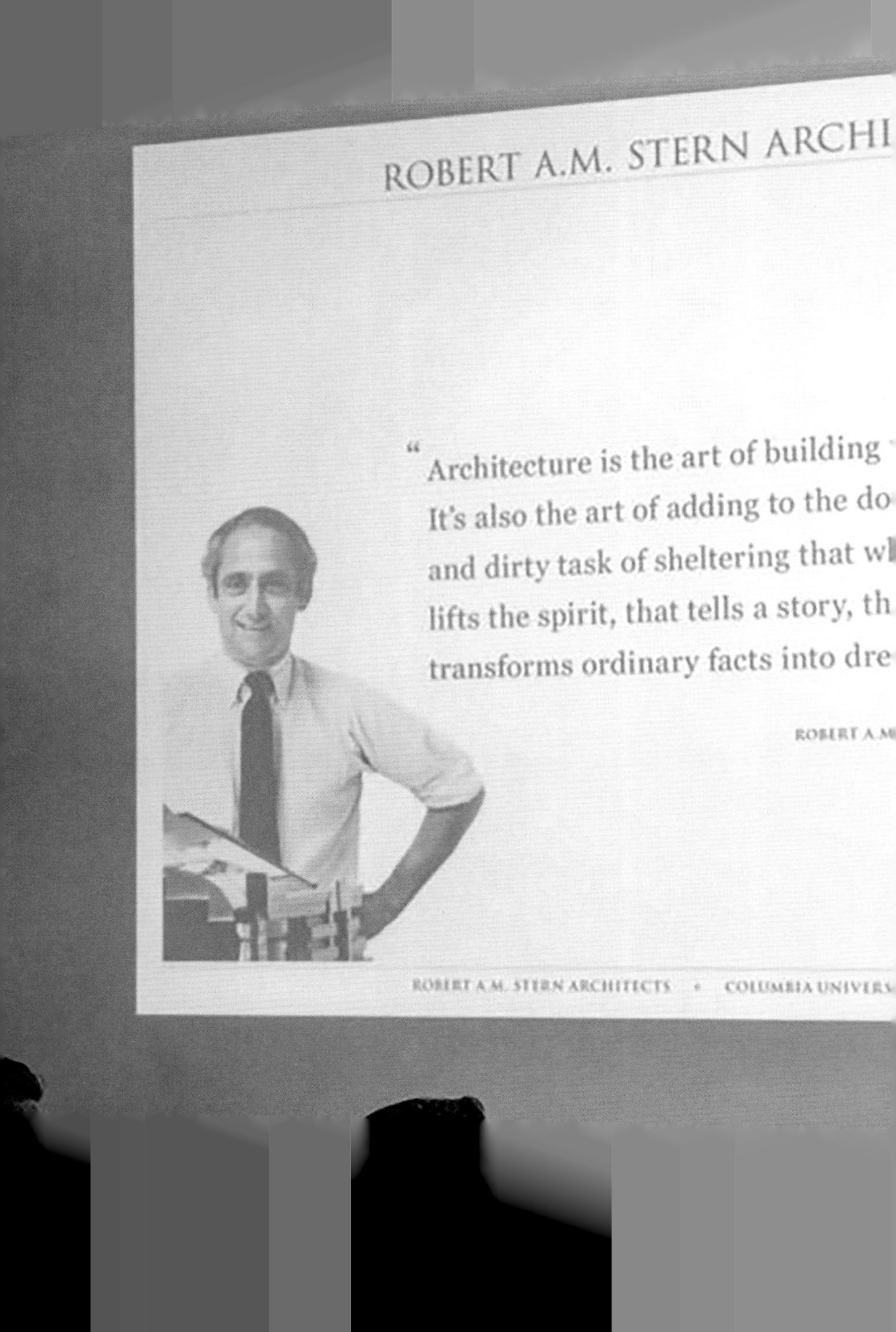
ROBERT A.M. STERN ARCHI
"Architecture is the art of building
It's also the art of adding to the do
and dirty task of sheltering that w
lifts the spirit, that tells a story, th
transforms ordinary facts into dre
ROBERT A.M
ROBERT A.M. STERN ARCHITECTS • COLUMBIA UNIVERS

In our work we rely on architectural principles of longstanding and fundamental importance because architecture, as a narrative art, must be legible to the users of a building. A welcoming entrance, a correspondence between inside and out, the accommodation of light and views: these are among the bases of our design thinking, the constants that underlie our work, no matter the mode of expression.

Each of our buildings presents a new opportunity to apply these principles to new situations, to different places, each with its own character. A building must enter into a conversation with its setting. If a building fits in, it will more than likely enjoy a long life—a connection to local history, the use of local materials, a composition that connects with the logic of its setting and does not hold itself aloof, that is one that deserves to endure, and will. Many of our buildings are in locations that are still in formation, and it is our hope that we are helping to lay the groundwork for the future.

WE BELIEVE IN OPEN SOCIETIES ORDERED BY MORAL CONVICTION. WE BELIEVE IN PRIVATE MARKETS, HUMANIZED BY COMPASSIONATE GOVERNMENT. WE BELIEVE IN ECONOMIES THAT REWARD EFFORT, COMMUNITIES THAT PROTECT THE WEAK, AND THE DUTY OF NATIONS TO RESPECT THE DIGNITY AND THE RIGHTS OF ALL.

President George W. Bush
Whitehall Palace, London. November 19, 2003

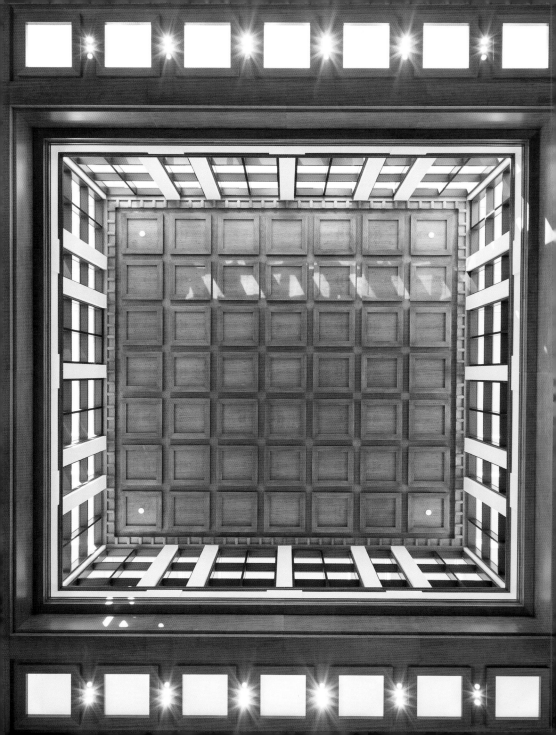

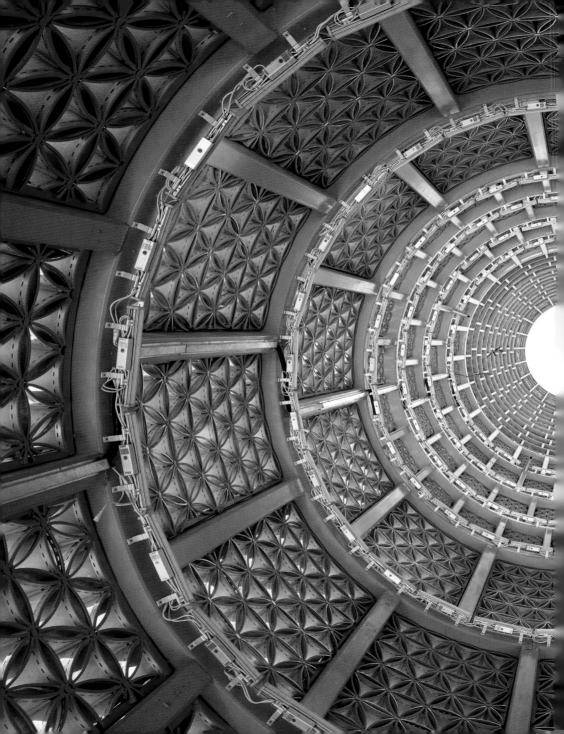

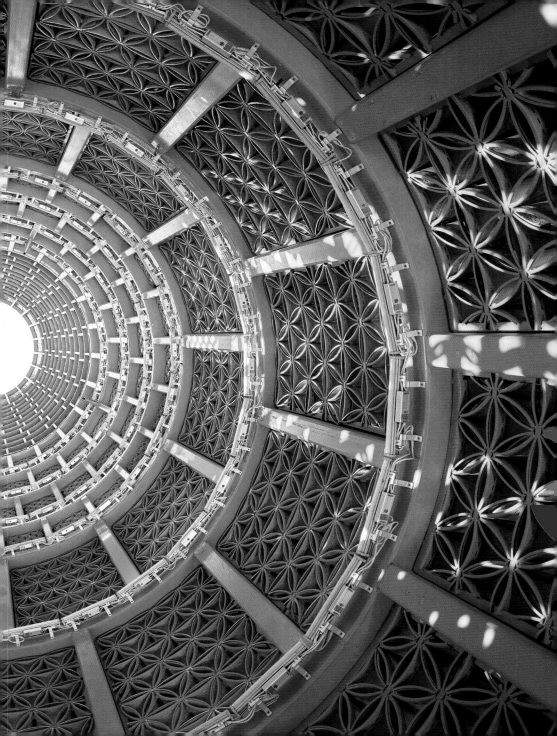

HENRICKSON
FAMILY ATRIUM

INMAN ADMISSIONS WELCOME CENTER

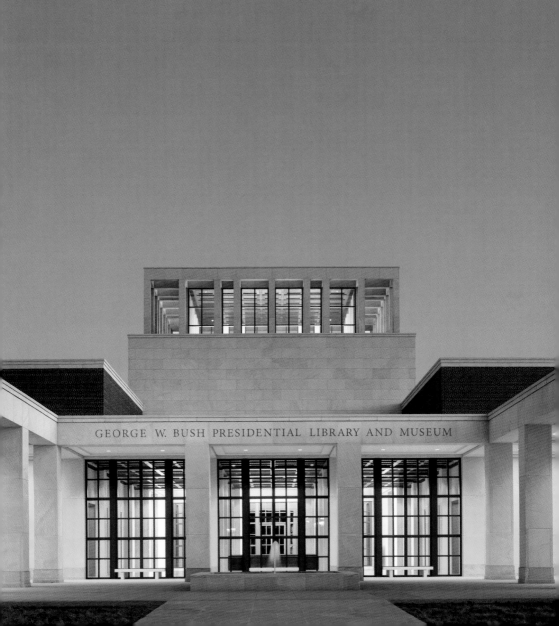

11
Elevation sketch
Robert A.M. Stern
Immanuel Chapel
Virginia Theological Seminary
Alexandria, Virginia

20
Faculty dining room sketch
Mason Roberts
Hoover Dining Hall
DePauw University
Greencastle, Indiana
21
"Tribute Tribune"
Matthew Roman

12–13
Concept sketch
Johnny Cruz
1468 Alberni Street
Vancouver, Canada

22–23
Crown study
Kevin M. Smith
Barkli Residence
Moscow, Russia

14
Concept sketch
Johnny Cruz
Residential Tower
Long Island City, New York
15
North Villa west elevation study
Tomasz Smierzchalski
Heart of Lake
Xiamen, China

24
Elevation sketch
Salvador E. Peña-Figueroa
Museum of the American Revolution
Philadelphia, Pennsylvania
25
Elevation sketches
Mason Roberts
Hubbard Center alterations
DePauw University
Greencastle, Indiana

16–17
Entry gate sketch
Randy M. Correll
Residence on Gin Lane
Southampton, New York

26–27
Stair sketches
Christian Dickson
East Hampton Town Hall
East Hampton, New York

18
North Villa east elevation studies
Tomasz Smierzchalski
Heart of Lake
Xiamen, China
19
Sketch for an ornamental panel
Brian F. Fell
Apartment at 15 Central Park West
New York, New York

28–29
Concept study
Christopher Heim
Hotel

30–31
North entry sketch
Caitlin M. Baransky
Sankey Hall
Elon University
Elon, North Carolina

40
Concept for a gateway
Matthew Cook
Poly Jinjiang Uptown
Jinjiang, China
41
Colonnade entry detail
David Pearson
Georgia Judicial Complex
Atlanta, Georgia

32–33
Business hotel front elevation
Huaxia Song
Liangjiang New District Town Center Center
Chongqing, China

42
Custom light fixture studies
Christopher Heim
Bavaro Hall
University of Virginia
Charlottesville, Virginia
43
Perspective study
Natalie Pierro
Residential Tower
Long Island City, New York

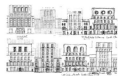

34–35
South elevation studies
Daniel Lobitz and Paul L. Whalen
30 Park Place
New York, New York

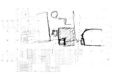

44–45
Floor plan
Robert A.M. Stern
Investment Company Offices
New York, New York

36
Concept sketch
Johnny Cruz
Residential Tower
Miami, Florida
37
Elevation sketch
Daniel Lobitz
30 Park Place
New York, New York

46–47
Perspective sketch
David Pearson
Residential Villa at Mountain Court
Hong Kong, China

38
Sketch plan
Daniel Lobitz
RAMSA Office
New York, New York
39
Terrace grading study
Natalie Ross
Residence
Martha's Vineyard,
Massachusetts

48
Entry design sketch
Caitlin M. Baransky
South Academy Street Residence Hall
University of Delaware
Newark, Delaware
49
Sketches of the health club
Ricardo Kendall
One Bennett Park
Chicago, Illinois

50–51
Entry motor court sketch
David Pearson
Hotel and Residential Tower
Texas

60–61
250 West 81st Street
New York, New York

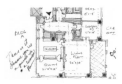

52–53
Sketch plan
Johnny Cruz
Residential Tower

62
Tour Carpe Diem
La Défense
Courbevoie, France
63
Offices for GlaxoSmithKline
Five Crescent Drive
The Navy Yard
Philadelphia, Pennsylvania

55
Dr. Phillips Academic Commons
University of Central Florida
Downtown Campus
Orlando, Florida

64–65
Museum of the American Revolution
Philadelphia, Pennsylvania

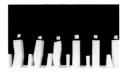

56–57
Studies for a tower
Philadelphia, Pennsylvania

66–67
Downtown Hartford Campus
University of Connecticut
Hartford, Connecticut

58
Studies for a tower
Philadelphia, Pennsylvania
59
Museum of the American Revolution
Philadelphia, Pennsylvania

68–69
Pauli Murray College and Benjamin Franklin College
Yale University
New Haven, Connecticut

70–71
One Water Street
Headquarters Building for
American Water
Camden, New Jersey

80–81
Residence in Edgartown
Martha's Vineyard,
Massachusetts

72–73
**Liangjiang New District
Town Center**
Chongqing, China

82–83
Immanuel Chapel
Virginia Theological Seminary
Alexandria, Virginia

74
520 Park Avenue
New York, New York
75
**Abington House
on the High Line**
New York, New York

85
Robert A.M. Stern, Chen-Huan
Liao, Daniel Lobitz, Sargent
C. Gardiner

76–77
**George W. Bush
Presidential Center**
Southern Methodist University
Dallas, Texas

86–87
Gelare Majidzadeh, Michael
D. Jones, Brenna Decker

78–79
**George W. Bush
Presidential Center**
Southern Methodist University
Dallas, Texas

88–89
Grant F. Marani, Robert A.M.
Stern, Charles H. Toothill II

90
Leopoldo Villardi, Robert
A.M. Stern
91
Gaylin M. Bowie

100–101
David Pearson

92
Top: Timothy S. Deal
Bottom: Johnny Cruz,
Shaohua Dong, Thomas Nye,
Tomasz Smierzchalski
93
Top: Allie Sutherland, Gary L.
Brewer, Matthew A. Blumenthal
Bottom: Leopoldo Villardi

102
Top: Thomas Day, Silas Jeffrey
Bottom: Robert A.M. Stern,
Mario Cruzate
103
Top: Kevin J. Kelly,
Edouard Terzis
Bottom: Kim S. Yap

94–95
Robert A.M. Stern, Alexander
P. Lamis

104–105
Paul L. Whalen, Georgina
Harvey, Grant F. Marani

96
Robert A.M. Stern
97
Johnny Cruz

106
Top: Caitlin M. Baransky
Bottom: Robert Moldafsky,
Katharine Gillis
107
Bina Bhattacharyya

98
Anya A. Grant,
Robert A.M. Stern
99
Patrick Corrigan, Huaxia Song,
Robert A.M. Stern

108–109
Charles H. Toothill II, Grant
F. Marani, Wenshu Xie, Robert
A.M. Stern, Joan Chen

110
Top: Jennifer Bailey, Preston
J. Gumberich, Carly Augustine
Bottom: Eric Dorsch, Michael
A. Weber
111
Top: Roger H. Seifter,
Eleanor Measham
Bottom: Randy M. Correll,
Megan St. Denis, Nicholas
Mingrone

120–21
Nadya Stryuk

112–13
Akshay Surana, Salvador
E. Peña-Figueroa, Rosalind
Tsang, Al Deliallisi

122
Tehniyet Masood, David
Abecassis
123
Marta Elliott, Tyler Nussbaum,
Luke Warren

114–15
Jennifer L. Stone, Graham
S. Wyatt

124–25
Paul L. Whalen, Natalie Pierro,
Georgina Harvey, Johnny Cruz

116
Niklas Thorsrud
117
Top: Robert A.M. Stern
Bottom: Robert A.M. Stern,
Kevin M. Smith, Kim S. Yap

126
Top: Daniel Lobitz
Bottom: Robert A.M. Stern
127
Top: Jonathan Kelly, Robert
A.M. Stern, Melissa DelVecchio,
Jennifer Bailey, Leo Stevens
Bottom: Robert A.M. Stern

118
Top: Graham S. Wyatt,
Kevin M. Smith
Bottom: Frederic J. Berthelot,
Daniel Lobitz, Meghan L.
McDermott, Robert A.M. Stern,
Kurt W. Glauber, Graham
S. Wyatt
119
Top: Boyuan Zhang,
Teddy Planitzer
Bottom: Robert A.M. Stern

128
Top: Michael McGrattan
Bottom: George de Brigard,
Lok Chan
129
Top: Mark Santrach
Bottom: Christopher Heim,
Robert A.M. Stern

130–31
Jules Gianakos, Cathryn Duffy, Anthony Sadler, Kimberly Taylor, Mark Santrach, David Pearson, Ian Spencer

140
Top: Marc Leverant, Jessie Turnbull, Kenan Wei, Tony McConnell, Timothy S. Deal, Rosalind Tsang
Bottom: Eric Dorsch, Hu Di
141
Top: RAMSA Summer Trip to Dupont Estates and Brandywine Valley
Bottom: Sam King

132
Top: Protest at 550 Madison Avenue, New York
Bottom: Brewer Studio New York Harbor cruise
133
Top: RAMSA gallery opening
Bottom: Runners in the JPMorganChase Corporate Challenge

142–43
Andrés Duany, Robert A.M. Stern

134
Top: Jan Lakin, Graham S. Wyatt, Robert A.M. Stern, Lisa Matkovic, Roger H. Seifter
Bottom: Natalie Pierro, Robert Cox, Melissa Duong
135
Top: Meghan L. McDermott, Frederic J. Berthelot
Bottom: Garry Novikoff, Peter Morris Dixon

144–45
Matthew Roman, Mary Burr, Paul L. Whalen, Conan Cassidy, Robert Cox, Marc DeSantis, Robert A.M. Stern

136–37
Grant F. Marani

146
Robert A.M. Stern, Melissa DelVecchio
147
Philip Chan, Robert A.M. Stern, Grant F. Marani, Paul G. Zembsch

138–39
C. Callaway Hayles, Kevin J. Kelly, Hu Di, Alexis Ryder, Kyung Sook Gemma Kim, Salvador E. Peña-Figueroa, Christopher Heim, David Pearson, Paul L. Whalen, Robert A.M. Stern

148
Top: Roger H. Seifter, Cara Timari, Ross Alexander
Bottom: Hernán R. Chebar, Michael D. Jones
149
Top: Silas Jeffrey, Donna Schragis
Bottom: Lauren Kruegel Siroky, Bruce Yao, Robert A.M. Stern, Paul L. Whalen

150–51
Mockups
Lancaster Avenue Housing
Villanova University
Villanova, Pennsylvania

160–61
C. Callaway Hayles
House in Virginia Beach
Virginia

152–53
Tim Wang, Bill Stein, Christine
Schwarzman, Stephen
A. Schwarzman, Melissa
DelVecchio, Robert A.M.
Stern, Chen Jining, Jonas
Goldberg, David Daokui
Li, at groundbreaking for
Schwarzman College, Tsinghua
University, Beijing

162
Top: Melissa DelVecchio,
Christopher McIntire, Zoltan
Kovacs, Graham S. Wyatt,
Kurt W. Glauber
Bottom: Brian Casey, Roger
H. Seifter
163
Top: Daniel Lobitz
Bottom: Robert A.M. Stern,
Daniel Lobitz

154
Mockup
Schwarzman College
Tsinghua University
Beijing, China
155
Mockup
Residence in the Northeast

164
Topping out ceremony
**Museum of the American
Revolution**
Philadelphia, Pennsylvania
165
Robert A.M. Stern, Paul
L. Whalen, Lima, Peru

156
Mockup
**Caruthers Biotechnology
Building**
University of Colorado
Boulder, Colorado
157
Mockup
**Pauli Murray College and
Benjamin Franklin College**
Yale University
New Haven, Connecticut

166
Site visit
**Pauli Murray College and
Benjamin Franklin College**
Yale University
New Haven, Connecticut
167
Tour of The Shed
New York

158–59
Mockup
One Bennett Park
Chicago, Illinois

168–69
Yang Bin, Qiu Yong, Melissa
DelVecchio

170–71
Robert A.M. Stern

180
House on Georgica Pond
Wainscott, New York
181
Residence on Nassim Road
Singapore

172
Robert A.M. Stern, Melissa
DelVecchio, Jonas Goldberg
173
Benchmarking tour

182–83
G. David Gearhart Hall
University of Arkansas
Fayetteville, Arkansas

174–75
Robert A.M. Stern
50 Connaught Road, Central
Hong Kong, China

184
Residence in East Quogue
East Quogue, New York
185
Mas Fleuri
St.-Jean-Cap-Ferrat, France

177
House
Glen Ellen, California

186
Mount Nicholson
Hong Kong, China
187
Residence on Gin Lane
Southampton, New York

178
Lovejoy Wharf
Boston, Massachusetts
179
The Morgan, 31 Conduit Road
Hong Kong, China

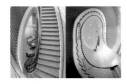

188
RAMSA Office
New York, New York
189
Residence in Montecito
Santa Barbara, California

190–91
Mount Nicholson
Hong Kong, China

200–201
Top: Mount Nicholson, Hong Kong; Residence in East Quogue, New York; Residence in the Northeast; House, Wainscott, New York. Bottom: Residence in East Quogue, New York; Residence on Martha's Vineyard; Residence in the Northeast

192–93
Top: House, Glen Ellen, California; 261 Hudson Street, New York; Tour Carpe Diem, La Défense; Residence, Southampton, New York. Bottom: Lovejoy Wharf, Boston; LeBow College of Business, Drexel University, Philadelphia; Mas Fleuri, St.-Jean-Cap-Ferrat; Gearhart Hall, University of Arkansas

202
Residence in East Quogue
East Quogue, New York
203
Residence on Gin Lane
Southampton, New York

194–95
Penthouse
Deer Valley, Utah

204
Residence in East Quogue
East Quogue, New York
205
House
Glen Ellen, California

196–97
2017 Kips Bay Decorator Show House
New York, New York

206
Pauli Murray College and Benjamin Franklin College
Yale University
New Haven, Connecticut
207
Arris
The Yards
Washington, D.C.

198–99
Fifth Avenue Apartment
New York, New York

208
Newell Hall
University of Florida
Gainesville, Florida
209
Chestnut Square
Drexel University
Philadelphia, Pennsylvania

210–11
George W. Bush
Presidential Center
Southern Methodist University
Dallas, Texas

220
George W. Bush
Presidential Center
Southern Methodist University
Dallas, Texas
221
Metropolis 79
Hangzhou, China

212
Farrell Hall, Wake Forest
School of Business
Wake Forest University
Winston-Salem, North Carolina
213
Howard L. Hawks Hall
College of Business
Administration
University of Nebraska
Lincoln, Nebraska

222–23
Top: Museum of the American
Revolution, Philadelphia;
Investment Company Offices,
New York. Bottom: Becker
Business Building, Florida
Southern College; 561 Avenida
Pezet, Lima, Peru

214–15
Offices for GlaxoSmithKline
Five Crescent Drive
The Navy Yard
Philadelphia, Pennsylvania

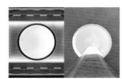

224
Barkli Residence
Moscow, Russia
225
Heart of Lake
Xiamen, China

216–17
Campus Transformation
Project
Harvard Kennedy School
of Government
Cambridge, Massachusetts

226–27
Poly Jinjiang Uptown
Jinjiang, China

218
Museum of the American
Revolution
Philadelphia, Pennsylvania
219
Schwarzman College
Tsinghua University
Beijing, China

228–29
Church of Jesus Christ
of Latter-day Saints
Meetinghouse
Philadelphia, Pennsylvania

230
Pauli Murray College and Benjamin Franklin College
Yale University
New Haven, Connecticut
231
Hoover Dining Hall
DePauw University
Greencastle, Indiana

240
Schwarzman College
Tsinghua University
Beijing, China
241
Chapel Hill Public Library
Chapel Hill, North Carolina

232–33
Music Addition, Rotunda, and Murray Student Center Renovation
Marist College
Poughkeepsie, New York

242–43
Immanuel Chapel
Virginia Theological Seminary
Alexandria, Virginia

234–35
George W. Bush Presidential Center
Southern Methodist University
Dallas, Texas

244–45
Top: Museum of the American Revolution, Philadelphia; McEwen School of Communications, Elon University, North Carolina. Bottom: Inman Admissions Welcome Center, Elon University, North Carolina; Music Addition, Marist College, Poughkeepsie, New York

236
Gerri C. LeBow Hall
LeBow College of Business
Drexel University
Philadelphia, Pennsylvania
237
Howard L. Hawks Hall
College of Business Administration
University of Nebraska
Lincoln, Nebraska

246–47
900 16th Street, NW
Washington, D.C.

238–39
Downtown Hartford Campus
University of Connecticut
Hartford, Connecticut

248–49
900 16th Street, NW
Washington, D.C.

250
Comcast Center
Philadelphia, Pennsylvania
251
Tour Carpe Diem
La Défense
Courbevoie, France

260–61
50 Connaught Road,
Central, Hong Kong, China

252–53
Tour Carpe Diem
La Défense
Courbevoie, France

262–63
Top: The Brompton, New
York; Lovejoy Wharf, Boston;
Mandarin Oriental, Atlanta;
The Westminster, New York.
Bottom: 900 16th Street, NW,
Washington, DC; 561 Avenida
Pezet, Lima, Peru; Win Sin Xin
Yi Residences, Taipei; The
Harrison, New York.

254–55
261 Hudson Street
New York, New York

264
375 Avenida Pezet
Lima, Peru

265
Barkli Residence
Moscow, Russia

256
**George W. Bush
Presidential Center**
Southern Methodist University
Dallas, Texas
257
Win Sing Xin Yi Residences
Taipei, Taiwan

266–67
900 16th Street, NW
Washington, D.C.

258–59
**Hong Kong Golf and
Tennis Academy**
Hong Kong, China

268–69
G. David Gearhart Hall
University of Arkansas
Fayetteville, Arkansas

270
Win Sing Xin Yi Residences
Taipei, Taiwan
271
**Inman Admissions
Welcome Center**
Elon University
Elon, North Carolina

280
**Pauli Murray College and
Benjamin Franklin College**
Yale University
New Haven, Connecticut
281
Immanuel Chapel
Virginia Theological Seminary
Alexandria, Virginia

272
**South Campus Housing,
West Quadrangle**
The University of South
Carolina
Columbia, South Carolina
273
Residence at West Tisbury
Martha's Vineyard,
Massachusetts

282
Residence
Salt Spring Island, British
Columbia
283
Emerald Riverside
Shanghai, China

274
Residence at West Tisbury
Martha's Vineyard,
Massachusetts
275
Residence in the Northeast

284–85
Residence in East Quogue
East Quogue, New York

276
Residence in the Northeast
277
**Abington House on the
High Line**
New York, New York

286
Win Sing Xin Yi Residences
Taipei, Taiwan
287
**George W. Bush
Presidential Center**
Southern Methodist University
Dallas, Texas

278
Ocean Course Clubhouse
Kiawah Island, South Carolina
279
Residence in East Quogue
East Quogue, New York

288–89
House
Glen Ellen, California

290
Schwarzman College
Tsinghua University
Beijing, China
291
Becker Business Building
Barney Barnett School of
Business
Florida Southern College
Lakeland, Florida

300–301
Heart of Lake
Xiamen, China

292
Immanuel Chapel
Virginia Theological Seminary
Alexandria, Virginia
293
**K.C. Irving Environmental
Science Centre**
and Harriet Irving Botanical
Gardens
Acadia University
Wolfville, Nova Scotia, Canada

302–303
House on Georgica Pond
Wainscott, New York

294–95
**Pauli Murray College and
Benjamin Franklin College**
Yale University
New Haven, Connecticut

304
**Hong Kong Golf and
Tennis Academy**
Hong Kong, China
305
The Morgan
31 Conduit Road
Hong Kong, China

296–97
**Pauli Murray College and
Benjamin Franklin College**
Yale University
New Haven, Connecticut

306-307
Residence at West Tisbury
Martha's Vineyard,
Massachusetts

298
Residence in the Northeast
299
Residence at West Tisbury
Martha's Vineyard,
Massachusetts

308-309
Residence on Nassim Road
Singapore

310–11
House on Georgica Pond
Wainscott, New York

320
Abington House on the High Line
New York, New York
321
Abington House on the High Line
New York, New York

312–13
Immanuel Chapel
Virginia Theological Seminary
Alexandria, Virginia

322–23
Damrak 70
Amsterdam, The Netherlands

314–15
Museum of the American Revolution
Philadelphia, Pennsylvania

324
Tour Carpe Diem
La Défense
Courbevoie, France
325
One Horizon Center
Gurgaon, Haryana, India

316
The Hewitt School
New York, New York
317
Heavener Hall
Warrington College of
Business Administration
University of Florida
Gainesville, Florida

326
Howard L. Hawks Hall
College of Business
Administration
University of Nebraska, Lincoln
Lincoln, Nebraska
327
Offices for GlaxoSmithKline
Five Crescent Drive
The Navy Yard
Philadelphia, Pennsylvania

318–19
Redlich Hall
The Hotchkiss School
Lakeville, Connecticut

328
900 16th Street, NW
Washington, D.C.
329
Downtown Hartford Campus
University of Connecticut
Hartford, Connecticut

330
375 Avenida Pezet
Lima, Peru
331
30 Park Place
New York, New York

340–41
Las Olas
Fort Lauderdale, Florida

332–33
Poly Jinjiang Uptown
Jinjiang, China

342–43
Pauli Murray College and Benjamin Franklin College
Yale University
New Haven, Connecticut

334–35
Mount Nicholson
Hong Kong, China

344–45
Chapel Hill Public Library
Chapel Hill, North Carolina

336–37
Residence at West Tisbury
Martha's Vineyard, Massachusetts

346–47
375 Avenida Pezet
Lima, Peru

338–39
Schwarzman College
Tsinghua University
Beijing, China

348
Howard L. Hawks Hall
College of Business Administration
University of Nebraska, Lincoln
Lincoln, Nebraska
349
Schwarzman College
Tsinghua University
Beijing, China

350–51
Dove Cottage
Lakeside, Michigan

360
Las Olas
Fort Lauderdale, Florida
361
Metropolis 79
Hangzhou, China

352
Stayer Center for Executive Education
Mendoza College of Business
University of Notre Dame
Notre Dame, Indiana
353
L. William Seidman Center
Seidman College of Business
Grand Valley State University
Grand Rapids, Michigan

362
Bedford Family Center
Westport Weston Family YMCA
Westport, Connecticut
363
George W. Bush Presidential Center
Southern Methodist University
Dallas, Texas

354
Hoover Dining Hall
DePauw University
Greencastle, Indiana
355
Terry College of Business
University of Georgia
Athens, Georgia

364–65
Barkli Residence
Moscow, Russia

356
Tour Carpe Diem
La Défense
Courbevoie, France
357
Offices for GlaxoSmithKline
Five Crescent Drive
The Navy Yard
Philadelphia, Pennsylvania

358–59
Metropolitan
Chongqing, China

Acknowledgments

We are grateful for the continuing support of our publisher, Gianfranco Monacelli, and for the editorial guidance of Elizabeth White and the production expertise of Michael Vagnetti. It has been a pleasure to collaborate again with graphic designer Michael Bierut of Pentagram and his colleague Laitsz Ho, who together worked to present our work in lively fashion. We also acknowledge the photographers— especially Peter Aaron, through whose eyes our completed projects are presented, and Bryan Coppede, who took many of the team photos that illustrate our process.

Photography Credits